Take-Off!

What are ...?
DESERTS

Andy Owen and
Miranda Ashwell

Heinemann
LIBRARY

First published in Great Britain by Heinemann Library
Halley Court, Jordan Hill, Oxford OX2 8EJ
a division of Reed Educational and Professional Publishing Ltd.
Heinemann is a registered trademark of Reed Educational and Professional Publishing Ltd.

OXFORD MELBOURNE AUCKLAND
IBADAN JOHANNESBURG BLANTYRE GABORONE
PORTSMOUTH NH (USA) CHICAGO

Designed by Susan Clarke and Celia Floyd
Illustrations by Oxford Illustrators (maps pp.23, 25, 27)
Originated by Dot Gradations, UK
Printed in Hong Kong/China

04 03 02 01 00
10 9 8 7 6 5 4 3 2 1

ISBN 0 431 02341 7

British Library Cataloguing in Publication Data

Owen, Andy
  What are deserts?. – (Take off!)
  1.Deserts – Juvenile literature
  I.Title II.Ashwell, Miranda III.Deserts
  551.4'15

Acknowledgements

The Publishers would like to thank the following for permission to reproduce photographs:
Barnaby's Picture Library p.21; Bill Bachman, pp.22, 24, 26; Bruce Coleman Ltd, p.13 (Gerald Cubitt), p.7 (Mr Jules Cowan), p.14 (David Hughes), p.9 (John Murray); FLPA, p.5 (W. Wisniewski), p.10 (Martin Withers); Magnum/Steve McCurry p.19; Oxford Scientific Films, p.11 (Marty Cordano), p.4 (Stan Osolinski); Planet Earth, p.29, pp.16, 18 (Thomas Dressler), p.6 (John Evans), p.12 (Peter Stephenson), p.17 (Ronald Rogott); Tony Stone, p.15 (Frank Heroldt), p.28 (Duncan Wherrett)

Cover photograph: Tony Stone/Paul Chesley

Our thanks to Sue Graves for her advice and expertise in the preparation of this book.

Every effort has been made to contact copyright holders of any material reproduced in this book. Any omissions will be rectified in subsequent printings if notice is given to the Publisher.

For more information about Heinemann Library books, or to order, please telephone +44(0)1865 888066, or send a fax to +44(0)1865 314091. You can visit our website at www.heinemann.co.uk

**This book is to be returned on or before
the last date stamped below.**

Contents

Some words are shown in bold, **like this**. You can find out what they mean by looking in the Glossary.

Deserts are dry

All deserts are dry. It may not rain for months or years. Few people can live in dry deserts.

This desert is sandy.

This desert is rocky.

Most deserts are rocky or stony places. Only special plants and animals can live where it is so dry.

A desert is a place where less than 25cms of rain falls in a year.

Flat and hilly deserts

Some deserts are flat so you can see a very long way. Crossing deserts can be difficult. People use camels to carry loads across deserts.

The Sahara Desert in Africa takes days to cross even when riding a camel.

Camels can go without water for days so they can live in deserts.

flat mountain tops

These desert mountains have flat tops.

Many deserts have rocky hills and mountains.
The wind carries sand across the open desert.
The sand cuts the rocks into odd shapes.

Hot and cold deserts

Some deserts get very hot.

mirage

The fierce heat plays tricks with the light. The hot ground can look like water but the water is not real. This is called a **mirage**.

The Atacama Desert is one of the coldest and driest deserts in the world.

Not all deserts are hot. The Atacama Desert in South America is one of the coldest deserts because it is so high up in the mountains.

The Atacama Desert has **droughts** for hundreds of years!

Days and nights

The desert sky often has no clouds. Without clouds in the way, the sun makes the ground very hot. Animals must shelter from the sun.

In a hot desert there are few places to shelter from the sun.

desert rats

Many animals sleep in the hot day and are awake at night.

Deserts become cold at night. There are no clouds to keep in the warmth of the day. Many animals are busy in the cool night. They come out from their shelters to look for food and drink.

Rain in the desert

In some deserts it only rains for a few hours each year. This is enough for some special plants to grow. **Cactus** plants grow well in the desert.

A cactus plant holds water in its stem to use when it is dry.

One of the driest places in the world is the
Namib Desert in Africa.

It may not rain in the driest deserts for many
years. The Namib Desert in Africa is a very dry
place. It is hard for anything to live there.

Desert storms

Strong winds whip the desert sand into the air. These **dust storms** can last for days. Small storms called **dust devils** last for a few minutes.

A dust devil is a small storm.

dust devil

These dark clouds show that a heavy thundery storm is about to start.

storm clouds

Most deserts have some rain in the year. The rain in the desert comes in heavy, thundery storms. They **flood** the land. Heavy rain washes away the sand.

Rivers in the desert

For most of the year this river is dry. It needs the rain to fill it with water. Without water you can see the **river bed**.

A dry river bed in the desert.

river bed

When it rains the river quickly fills with water. It rains for a short time so the river will only flow for a few hours. Soon the river will be dry again.

This river will only flow for a few hours.

The moving desert

The tops of sand **dunes** are called crests. The wind carries sand over the crest and drops it on the other side. The wind blows the sand into many shapes.

The desert wind blows the sand into beautiful shapes called dunes.

These people are trying to get the sand out of their home.

Wind and **dust storms** blow the desert sands across roads and into buildings. It can be hard to get desert sand out of homes and buildings.

19

Water in the desert

Without water people cannot live in the desert.
Water can be found in a few special places.
These special places are called **oases**.

People will travel for days to get water
from this **oasis** in the desert.

oasis

Phoenix is a desert city in America. People in Phoenix use water in their homes and gardens. The water comes from under the ground.

Water used in Phoenix comes from under the ground and from a river many kilometres away.

Desert map 1

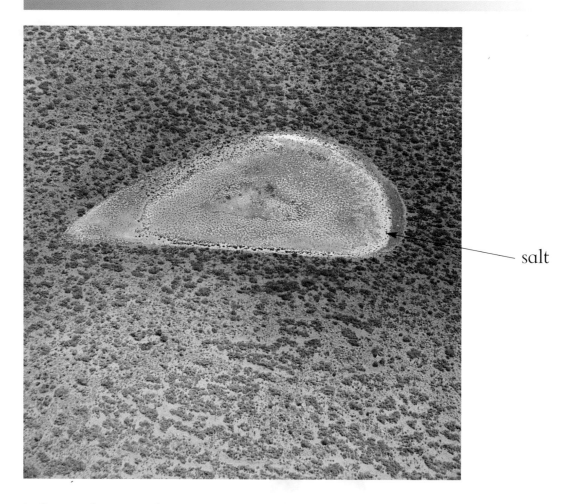

salt

This photo shows part of a sandy desert in Australia. The pear shape is where water has been dried up by the hot sun. You can see salt that has been left behind after the water has gone.

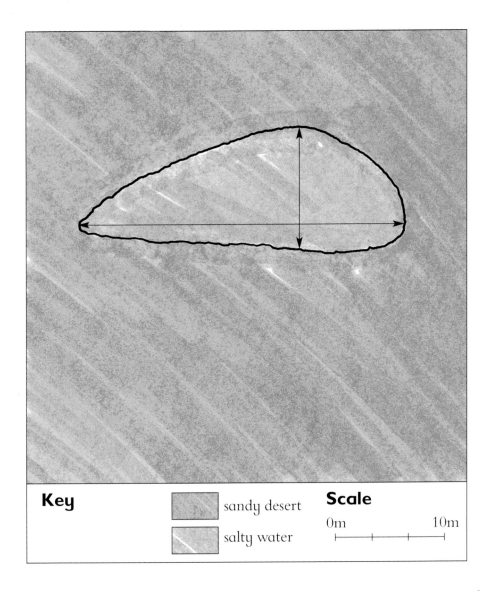

This map uses colours to show the same place as the photo. The orange colour shows the sandy desert. The grey colour tells us that any water here will be salty. Measure the water hole. Read the scale to work out how big the water hole is.

Desert map 2

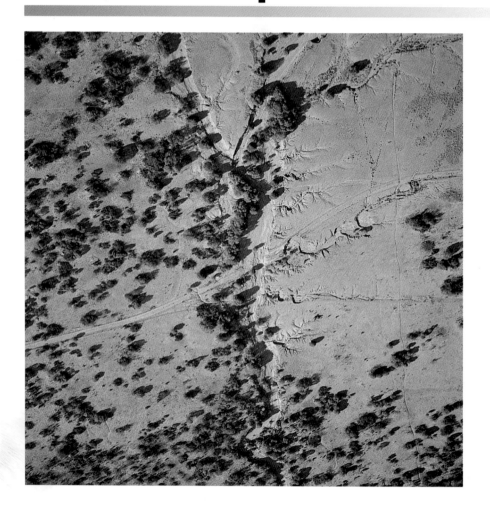

This photo is of a dirt road which crosses the desert in Australia. The road crosses a river. There is no bridge because the river is dry for most of the year.

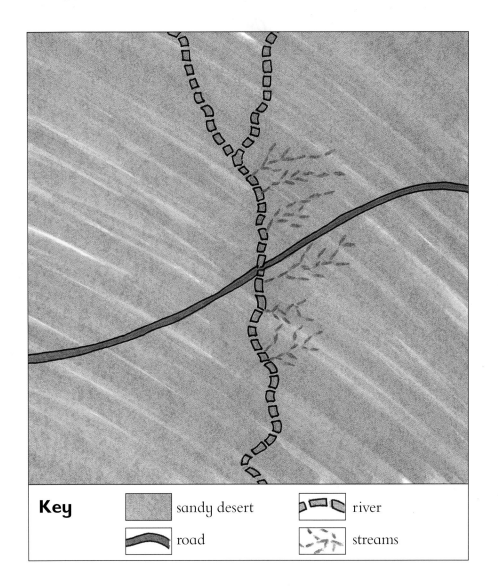

Key

sandy desert	river
road	streams

Rivers are shown on maps with a blue line. This river is shown with a broken blue line. This tells us that the river is normally dry. Using the map key, find the river, the streams and the road.

Desert map 3

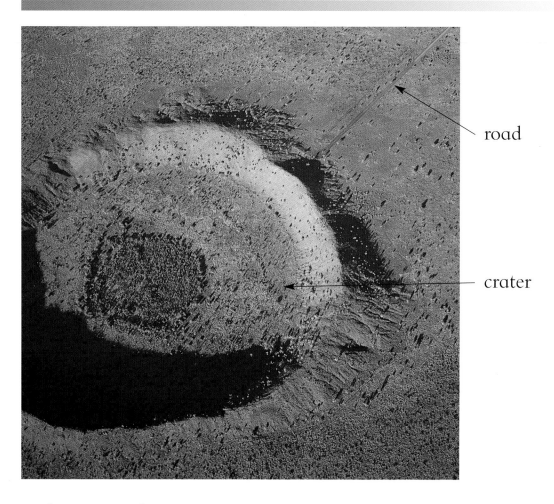

road

crater

A huge rock from space landed in the desert a long time ago. It made a big hole called a **crater**. A road has been built so that people can come to see the crater.

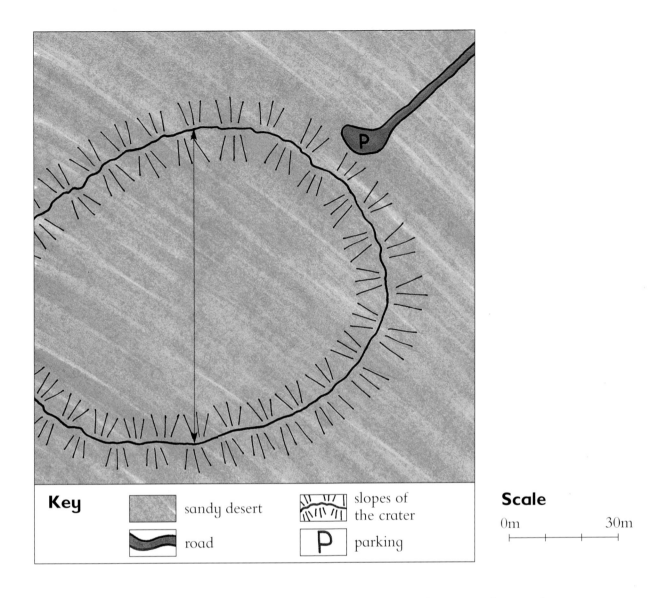

Key
| | sandy desert |
| | road |
| slopes of the crater |
| P | parking |

Scale

0m   30m

People who visit the crater, park at the end of the road. They walk up the steep slope of the crater and then down into the middle. Use the scale to work out how wide the crater is.

Amazing desert facts

The Sahara Desert in Africa is the biggest desert in the world. This desert is nearly as big as the United States of America.

Most of the Sahara Desert is rocky. Only about one-tenth is sand.

The biggest **dunes** in the world are in the Namib Desert in Africa. The shape and size of the dunes can change as the wind changes its direction.

Glossary

cactus a desert plant

crater a large hole formed by an explosion

droughts long periods of time with no rain

dunes hills made out of sand

dust devils short storms that pick up sand

dust storms when strong winds whip the desert sand into the air. This can last for several days

flood water from a river that spills onto the land

mirage when the hot air plays tricks with the light. For example, roads and sand can look as if they are covered in water

oasis (plural **oases**) a place where you can find water in the desert

river bed the bottom of a river

More books to read

Nicola Baxter. *Our Wonderful Earth.*
Two-Can, 1997

Claire Llewellyn. *Why do we have?
Deserts and Rainforests.*
Heinemann Library, 1997

Joy Palmer. *First Starts: Deserts.*
Franklin Watts, 1996

Neil Morris. *The World's Top Ten Deserts.*
Belitha Press, 1996

Index